First Edition
ISBN 9798387655661

THIS COLORING BOOK BELONGS TO:

....

COLOR TEST PAGE

KEEP
CALM
AND
CARRY
THE F*CK
ON!

CHEER
THE
F*CK
UP!

BE
AWESOME
AND
GIVE NO
F*CKS

I PLAY
WITH MY
F*CKING
RULES

YOU ARE
AWESOME
AS
F*CK!!

F*CK
REALITY

SHIT
HAPPENS

LET
SHIT
THAT
GO

F*CKING
AWESOME

I CAN
AND I
F*CKING
WILL

BASIC
B*TCH

BE HAPPY
IT
DRIVES
ASSHOLES
CRAZY!

STOP
HOARDING
EVERYTHING
ASSHOLE!

KEEP
THAT
SHiT
UP

FRESH
OUT
OF
F*CK

KEEP
F*CKING
PUSHING
FORWARD

YOU'RE
A
MOTHER
F*CKING
BADASS

I CAN
F*CKING
DO
THIS

CHASE
YOUR
F*CKING
DREAM

MAKE
EVERY
DREAM
MOMENT
COUNT

NEVER
QUIT,
ONLY
REST
BITCHES!

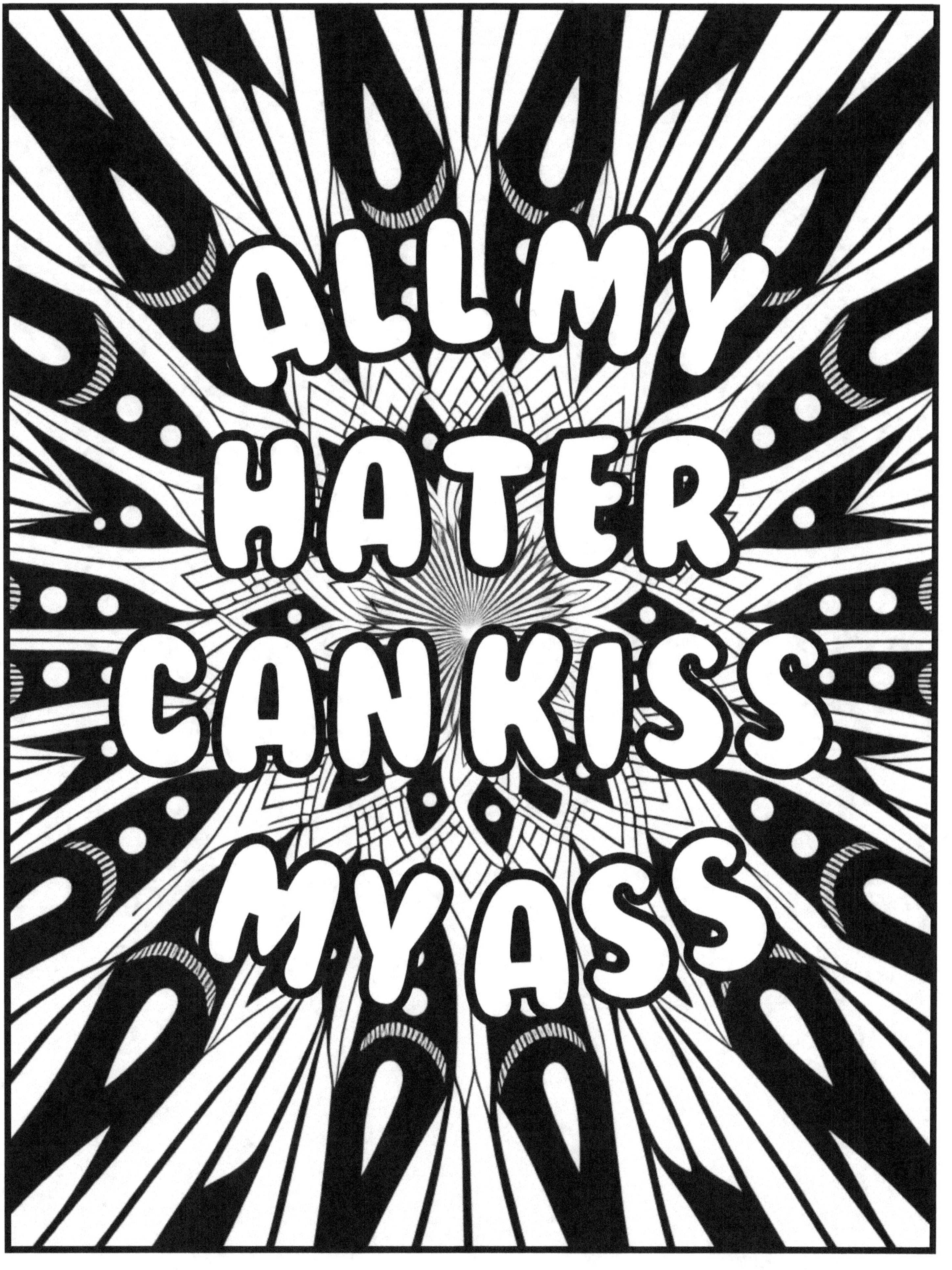
ALL MY
HATER
CAN KISS
MY ASS

GOOD
F*CKING
VIBES
ONLY

NEVER
GIVE
THE
F*CK UP

DREAM
BIG
ACHIEVE
MORE

DREAM
SO DAMN
BIG
YOUR HATER
ASK IF
YOU'RE HIRING

LIFE IS
TOO DAMN
SHORT
GO AFTER
YOUR
DREAM

CHILL
THE
F*CK
OUT

F*CK
THE
HATER

BELIEVE
IN YOUR
DAMN
POTENTIAL

WALK
IN YOUR
DAMN
PURPOSE

YOU'RE
AMAZING
AS F*CK
KEEP
THAT SHIT
UP

WAKE UP
KICK ASS
REPEAT

IF YOU
F*CK WITH
MY PEACE,
I'LL CUT
A BITCH

I'M NOT
ANTI
SOCIAL,
I'M ANTI
BULLSHIT

THE
FUTURE
IS
F*CKING
BRIGHT

IF IT WAS
EASY
EVERY
DUMBASS
WOULD
DO IT

THERE ARE
NO LIMITS
TO THE
AMAZING
SHIT
THAT I CAN DO

HONESTLY
AS LONG AS
YOU'RE
HAPPY
WHO
THE HELL
CARES!

TODAY'S GOING
TO BE
A GOOD
F*CKING DAY.
THINK
POSITIVE!

DON'T
FEEL SORRY
FOR YOURSELF.
ONLY A**HOLES
DO THAT!!

INHALE
THE GOOD
SHIT

EXHALE
THE BAD
SHIT

I GOT THIS
SHIT

F*CK
WHAT
THEY
THINK

MAKE
EACH DAY
YOUR
MASTERPIECES

DON'T MAKE ME
USE MY
F*CKING
AWESOME

YOU'RE
F*CKING
MAGICAL

B!ITCH
DØN'T
KILL
MY VIBE

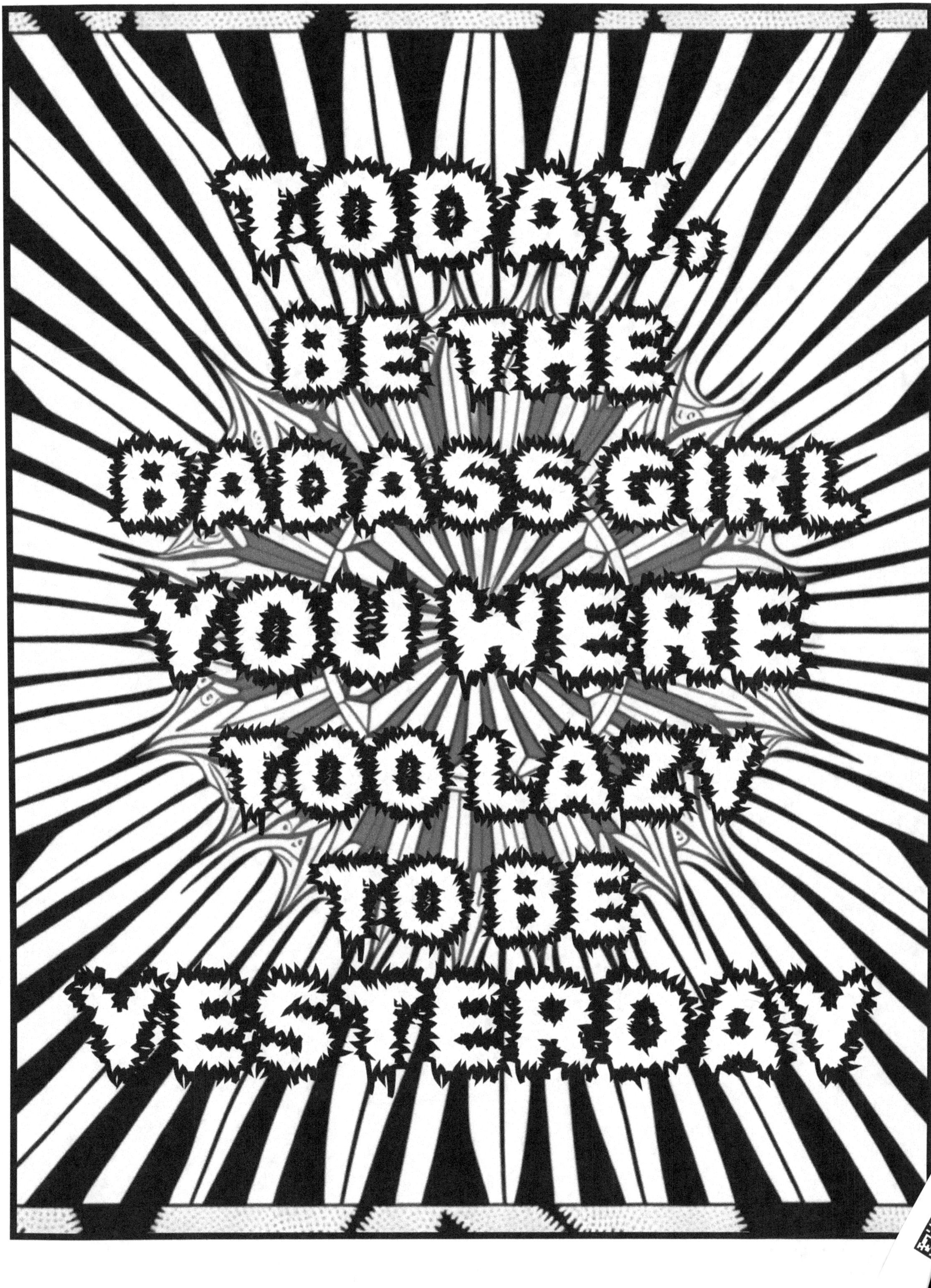
TODAY,
BE THE
BADASS GIRL
YOU WERE
TOO LAZY
TO BE
YESTERDAY

www.ingramcontent.com/pod-product-compliance
Lightning Source LLC
Chambersburg PA
CBHW082147230526
45467CB00043B/2404
* 9 7 9 8 3 8 7 6 5 5 6 6 1 *